A I

CW00411167

SOUTHWOLD
WALBERSWICK,
BLYTHBURGH
AND
DUNWICH

TERRY PALMER

HERITAGE
HOUSE

A DAY OUT IN SOUTHWOLD...
First published June 1994
Completely revised 2nd edition May 2001
ISBN 185215.0882.
Printed by Hythe Offset, Colchester
Published by Heritage House

Heritage House (Publishers) Ltd,
Steam Mill Road, Bradfield, MANNINGTREE, C011 2QT
www.heritage-house.co.uk
e-mail: sales@heritage-house.co.uk

Heritage House publishes walkers' maps and tourist guides to East Anglia.

Special thanks for the photography to **Richard Wells** of Southwold and to all the people of the area who have helped with research.

The symbol ❀ indicates something worth seeing.

COVERS:
Front: St James's Green and Southwold lighthouse.
Rear: A stormy day at Southwold beach.

WELCOME!

WELCOME to a part of Suffolk where life, on the surface, is still lived as it used to be. The only town is quiet, peaceful, unspoiled, and as full of character as it is empty of tower blocks. There are no traffic jams on the country lanes and few in the town itself; as I write there are no traffic lights - oh, happy day! - and not too many yellow lines on the roads.

There is no longer a railway, but train fanatics can trace its course through Blythburgh and Walberswick to Southwold, but not to Dunwich.

The four communities have three large churches, two with a wall-mounted mannikin who strikes the hours and is sometimes called Jack-o'-the-Clock, the third has been roofless for centuries with a smaller church sitting in its original nave, and the fourth community once had nine churches.

In Southwold there is a beautiful lighthouse that cries out to be photographed, and there are cannon which have been sitting on a clifftop for four centuries, waiting for an enemy who never comes.

There is a tiny village that was once a city, a Roman port, the capital of eastern England, a bishopric, and which sent two Members to Parliament.

This part of Suffolk appeals to lovers of life as it used to be; there are no acres of holiday caravans, no fairgrounds, no miles of bright lights and no bingo. Welcome to a bit of peace and quiet!

A DAY OUT IN SOUTHWOLD,
Walberswick, Blythburgh and Dunwich

WHEN YOU REACH the heart of Southwold your eye will be torn between the lighthouse, the church, and the Georgian architecture around the Market Place. But beware your eyes don't deceive you!

Lighthouse. Let's look first at the ❀ lighthouse, that dazzling white tower rising from the highest point in town and still showing its occulting beacon (dark intervals longer than its light ones) as it has done since 1890, the year after work began on the tower. The engineer-in-chief of the project was also in charge of building the beacons at Cromer and Hunstanton. As all three are in use you're normally not allowed to climb them but take my word; there are 120 steps.

Harwich-based Trinity House runs all the navigation lights and marks around the coast of England, Wales, the Channel Islands and Gibraltar, as well as all the buoys and the LANBYs - Large Automatic Navigational Beacons - that have replaced the lightships.

St Edmund's Church. I named the ❀ church as the second landmark you will see. It stands in its own churchyard and is dominated by its massive square tower, 100 feet tall. When was it built? Work could have begun in 1413, the year Henry V came to the throne, but some authorities date the start in the reign of Henry VI, from 1422 to 1461, but it's reckoned to have been finished in 1460.

It's now claimed to be the best Medieval church in an English coastal town.

Edward VI's royal arms, the swan and the ermine, are carved in a window mullion to remind us that he was Lord of the Manor of Southwold, but so too was Henry IV, the first of the House of Lancaster, who reigned from 1399 to 1413. The work almost certainly ended in 1482, but Henry VII, the first of

Southwold Jack - but not the real one

the Tudors, granted Southwold its first charter in 1489.

❀ **Southwold Jack.** While the Wars of the Roses were continuing, from 1455 to 1486, somebody carved a half-lifesized model of a soldier dressed in contemporary uniform, and fixed him comfortably above head height on the nave wall at Southwold; there was a similar one, called ❀ Jack-o'-the-Clock, in the church at Blythburgh. Both these interesting characters are still in working order more than five centuries after they were erected, a compliment to workmanship. A sidesman at Southwold pulls a rope and Jack hits a bell with his battleaxe to announce the start of the service. The Jacks are so good that Shakespeare could have heard of them, because he wrote in Richard I, "I stand fooling here like Jack o' the Clock."

Another compliment is due for the intricate work of St Edmund's ❀ font cover, standing 24 ft tall, like a Concorde nose cone at attention. It's claimed to be the tallest in Britain but it's a replica built in 1935 because William Dowsing, Cromwell's minion, destroyed the original.

Haile Selassie. You've heard of the last Emperor of Abyssinia, now Ethiopia? His family gave the processional cross which stands near the ✿ East Window. The window itself, designed in 1954, shows **Saint Edmund** about to be killed by arrows. He was one of the Saxon kings of East Anglia and was murdered by invading Danes in 870.

Mausoleum. I began with a warning: don't let your eyes deceive you. Remember that if you stand on the south side of the church and look at the inscription on William Bardwell's mausoleum. Bardwell was a local architect with big ideas. He designed a fanciful Town Hall for Southwold, then went on to plan an even more fanciful House of Commons. Neither was built, so poor Bardwell's mausoleum is his main monument to success.

From the churchyard you can see that the original road into town forked left at North Green and headed straight for St Edmund's west door but, as commercial interests overtook religious ones, traffic went down today's High Street to the ✿ Market Place. Not surprising when we learn that this church, grand though it may be, was until 1751 the chapel of ease for St Margaret's Church in Reydon.

Reydon. And that prompts an explanation for the origins of the town. Southwold began in Saxon times as a few fishing huts on an island formed by the Blyth River and the smaller Buss Creek cutting north-eastward; you still have to cross the creek to reach the town. The fishermen lived on the slightly higher land at Reydon, a part of town which is now totally bypassed by tourists.

The Domesday record of 1086 states that Reydon had to send 25,000 herring a year to St Edmund's Abbey at Bury, which owned the manorial rights. Then in 1202 the Bishop of Norwich, John de Grey, received Papal permission for the Cluniac priors of Thetford to build a chapel on the island, which was to be dedicated to St Edmund. De Grey's chapel lasted for around 200 years, and its foundations were discovered in 1758 under the chancel of St Edmund's Church; we've seen that the present church was begun soon after de

Grey's chapel hit the dust.

A Bit of Background. Here's some background information. In Roman times and for long after, Dunwich was the most important community in the Eastern Counties. The first bishop of the entire region, Felix - you can guess which town takes his name - was based in Dunwich from 631, but around 680 the territory was split into two bishoprics - sees - based on what had been the nordfolk and the sudfolk, the first division of the original Angle settlers. The northern see was based at North Elmham, between Fakenham and Dereham, until the Vikings killed Edmund. This northern see was abandoned, to be reinstated at Thetford in 1071. In that same year Dunwich lost its Episcopal position in favour of Bury St Edmunds, but in 1085 both towns were downgraded in favour of Norwich. So now you know.

The Great Fire. Remember that warning about not always believing your eyes? The coastal end of Southwold's High Street and around the Market Square has a good display of Georgian architecture, particularly noticeable in the windows. In 1659 a fire started on East Cliff and was swept into town by a sea wind. It destroyed 238 houses, the Town Hall, the Jail, the Market

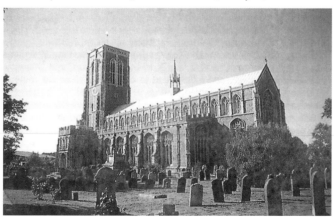

St. Edmund's Church, Southworld

House, numerous shops and several breweries, and the ❀ Swan Hotel - in fact, almost the entire town except for the church and Sutherland House.

Greens. Rebuilding began soon after, the Swan emerging from the ashes soon after 1660, but the town planners decided they didn't want to risk another conflagration so they left several empty areas as firebreaks. Today they're known as the ❀ greens, and there are nine of them: North Green, the first you see; the small Barnaby Green; Bartholomew Green near the museum; Church Green; St Edmund's Green east of the church; East Green; Tibby's Green, west of the church; St James's Green near the lighthouse; and South Green overlooking Gun Hill. Bartholomew's Green had been the site of Bartholomew's Fair for centuries, so presumably it had always been an open space? There's no way of knowing as the town's records were lost in the blaze.

Sutherland House. Thomas Camel was an early owner of ❀ Sutherland House, a relation of one Anne Camel who was found not guilty of witchcraft in 1649 and so escaped a nasty execution. Dr John Sutherland, a marine surgeon, owned the house and practised here from 1808 and it was from him that the name originated. The place is part-open to the public as it's a restaurant, but its greatest claim to fame is that the Duke of York, Lord High Admiral of England, brother of Charles II, made his headquarters in Sutherland House during the Anglo-Dutch Wars, including the **Battle of Sole Bay**. Matthew Wren, brother of the architect Sir Christopher, was here at the time: he wrote a detailed report to Whitehall of the battle. So we'd better talk about it as I'm certain you've never heard of it - unless you've read the plaque outside Sutherland House (see below).

Battle of Sole Bay. You've probably never heard of the bay, either: it's between Walberswick and Dunwich and is very shallow - but it was deeper in 1672 before the headlands at Easton Ness and Dunwich eroded. The battle is even more difficult to find; it's in a few obscure history books, but the greatest explanation is to be found in the ✿ **Southwold Museum** and its private library.

In 1668 England, Sweden, and the United Provinces - Wallonia and the Netherlands - formed the Triple Alliance and forced France's Louis XIV to make peace with Spain. But in 1672 England allied herself with France and was fighting against the United Provinces in the Third Anglo-Dutch War. Why, for heaven's sake? England decided it was important to check the growing Dutch commercial threat, and France wanted to hurt Spain which still had interests in the Spanish Netherlands where it didn't belong. The Dutch (with Spanish backing) were trying to avoid a French victory on land but they (and the English) suspected Louis XIV had ordered his vice-admiral the Compte d'Estrées to go easy on the amateurs manning the French ships. The Dutch commander, Admiral Michiel de Ruyter, an ancestor of the man who created Reuter's Press Agency, held his ground aboard the 80-gun *Zeven*

Sutherland House, Southwold, has plenty to say about the Battle of Sole Bay.

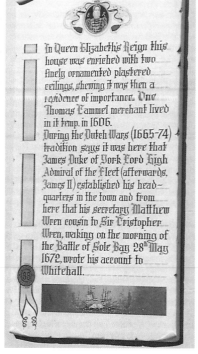

In Queen Elizabeth's Reign this house was enriched with two finely ornamented plastered ceilings, shewing it was then a residence of importance. One Thomas Cammel merchant lived in it temp. in 1606.
During the Dutch Wars (1665-74) tradition says it was here that James Duke of York Lord High Admiral of the Fleet (afterwards, James II) established his head-quarters in the town and from here that his secretary Matthew Wren cousin to Sir Cristopher Wren, waking on the morning of the Battle of Sole Bay 28ᵗʰ May 1672, wrote his account to Whitehall.

9

Provincien and saw the Allies retreat. To Sole Bay, where they arrived on Whit Monday.

Why Sole Bay? Because the Duke of York had made Sutherland House his HQ for the two earlier Anglo-Dutch wars, and the English captain came here for orders. But on the morning of 28 May, 1672, Whit Sunday, while the fleets were anxiously holding their positions against a lee shore, a French lookout saw the first of the 74 Dutch ships bearing down from the east-nor'-east in line abreast, with 36 fireships - and the wind from the east-sou'-east.

Immediate action was needed. The English and the French had men ashore getting water and so, with reduced crews and a lee shore, the 98 Allied ships and 30 fireships hauled anchors or cut cables and sailed. The French went south-east, their ships, including the *Terrible* of 70 guns, *St Phillippe* with 78, *Foudroyant* with 70 and *Tonnant* with just 58, exchanged long-range cannon fire with a Dutch squadron, and were thereafter *hors de combat*.

Rear Admiral Sir John Harman in *Royal Charles* commanded the Red, while the Duke of York led the White Squadron from the 100-gun *Royal Prince*. Five Dutch ships attacked the *Royal James*, a 100-gun man-o'-war flying the standard of the First Earl of Sandwich, commander of the Blue Squadron.

Sandwich. Earl Montagu, the first earl, was an early victim of the battle when *Royal James* was sunk; his body was washed ashore near Harwich. This earl was great-grandfather to the man who put meat between two slices of bread and so invented convenience food.

Landguard. The battle was fought out of sight of the coast yet was heard for miles inland, but some confusion exists, as I have seen the original letter from *Landguard Fort, May 28, '72 Tuesday evening 8 a clock* which claims *I am just come from Aldborow where...I found the fleets ingaged.*

The final twist in the tale came when the Duke of York,

The Battle of Sole Bay, by courtesy of Southwold Museum

now crowned James II, fled to France while his throne went to William of Orange - a Dutchman.

Adnams. The Sole Bay brewery was alive and well in 1641 - and probably earlier - so it predated fire and battle. It was probably behind the Swan Hotel in the town centre; in 1872 it was still a small business in the corner of the yard when the Adnams family bought it and began expanding. Soon the company was buying up the opposition and winning awards, brewing with Suffolk barley and Kentish hops.

Adnams is still a small firm compared with the brewing giants, but it has 70 pubs in the area and a range of popular brews, which makes it the best-known business in the town. Its horse-drawn drays, reintroduced in 1970, help with publicity. Among its watering holes are the ❀ *Sole Bay*; the *Lord Nelson*; the *Harbour Inn* where the landlord and six others were marooned for a day by the 1953 floods; the *Swan Hotel*; and the *Queen's Head* at Blyford, used by smugglers - their goods were hidden in the parish church in desperate times.

Tunnels. You won't hear much about the tunnels that run under High Street and possibly between the church and Gun Hill. The tale that they were used by smugglers is probably far-

11

fetched, but you can take it as fact that some of them exist: I've been in one, but not even the excise men will force me to reveal where.

Gun Hill. If there is a tunnel to ✿ Gun Hill, its entry is carefully hidden. The town faces a hostile sea, from which Dutch and French vessels could strike - and have struck - and from which the Danes and Vikings had struck in earlier centuries. Strange, then, that the town had no defences until 1569 when the Earl of Warwick gave eight cannon on condition that Southwold provided the gunpowder. It wouldn't, so the guns either never came or they went away.

Sir Robert Wingfield ordered the corporation to obey, in 1580, but again it refused. Seven years later, with the threat of the Spanish Armada looming, a Captain Turner surveyed the town and decided it was "weak, but strongly situated". He send eight guns to defend the north flank and others for the south, but after the Spaniards sailed by (they were, after all, a defeated rabble) the guns were left to rust.

Duke of Cumberland. Controversy intervenes yet again in the town's history. Some sources claim that the Duke of Cumberland, known as Butcher Cumberland after his slaughter of the Highland troops at the Battle of Culloden Moor on 16 February 1746, gave the town six eighteen-pound ✿ Elizabethan cannon captured at the battle, with forty cannonballs for each, but historian P J Macksey claims the Board of Ordnance made the gift. It is fact that the corporation accepted them and set them up where they stand today - on Gun Hill.

Most of them were fired to mark the birthday of the then Prince of Wales on 9 November 1842, but when Jimmy Martin's gun refused to fire he went around and peered in the barrel to see why. It fired, taking his head off - and the ordnance hasn't been used since.

Casino. South of the cannon stands a strange building, erected in 1800 as a reading-room or a casino, a queer mixture.

The builder of this octagonal edifice, James Thompson, died in 1806, after which a group of locals bought the lease of the casino and surrounding land to make sure there were no further weird constructions. From June to September it is also the ❀ **RNLI Museum**, featuring the collection of former councillor John Goldsmith and the town's lifeboat, now replaced by an inshore rescue launch.

❀ **Sailors' Reading Room.** There's another reading-room in town, at East Cliff. It was built in 1846 for £546, not including the plot. Mrs Rayley had it built in memory of her husband, Captain Charles, to deter sailors and fishermen from spending too much time and money in the local pubs. She also provided entertainment and the beginnings of a nautical museum which now has several carved figureheads among its exhibits; it's open to the public.

Water tower. Until 1991 the RNLI Museum was in the old metal water tower on York Road, which was renovated in 1998. The town lost another unusual building, the Kipperdrome, in the 1920s; it was a circular fishmarket on the site of toilets for a caravan park.

Castle. Southwold even had a castle. It stood in the Constitution Hill area, near South Green, and was the work of the Earl of Clare in 1259. The Clares were important folk; in addition to this castle they built one in Clare, Suffolk, others at Aberystwyth and Cardiff. They were responsible for Tintern Abbey, they established Clare County in Ireland, and rescued University College in Cambridge to re-establish it under their name.

❀ **Town Museum.** The Town Museum in Victoria St stands in two back-to-back Dutch-style cottages built soon after the fire, and due for demolition in 1933 but presented to the town instead by Mrs Goddard, wife of a garage proprietor. It is now a storehouse of fossils, and memorabilia on the Battle of Sole Bay and the Southwold Railway.

❀ **Town Pump.** The pump has stood in the middle of the

market place since 1873, with cast iron herring forming the main motif. Made in the town, it stands on the site of the market cross which lived here from 1666 to 1809; typical of other market crosses in East Anglia, it had market traders on the ground and a corporation office upstairs.

There was a jail on the eastern side of the market place. The cells are now used as storage by the shop on the site. Henry VII gave the jail its charter but it was abandoned in 1835, shortly after a prisoner escaped within minutes of being slammed up. He climbed over the rear wall!

Go down Queen St and you will find May Place, a house once owned by Admiral Edward **Vernon**, whose main abode was the vast manor of Orwell Park in Nacton, on the Orwell estuary. Vernon made his fortune by raiding ports in Spain, Portugal and Brazil, but he made his reputation by watering his sailors' rum ration. His trade mark clothing was a cloak of corded silk, called gros grain - coarse thread - which the matelots called grogram. Soon they called his rum by the same name, shortening it to grog.

Grog Vernon was involved with the Free British Fishery which revived interest in making sea salt by dehydration in

Walberswick harbour.

shallow lagoons on Southwold marshes; it continued until around 1894.

Among the locals gathering salt tax was a member of the **Strickland** family. A successor, Agnes Strickland, was a local historian and novelist, whose books included *The Lives of the Queens of England* and the fictional *How Will It End?* She died at her Lorne Road home in 1874.

Artists and Writers. Stanley Spencer, painter of religious subjects and WW2 military actions - a bizarre mixture - visited Southwold and Walberswick without producing much of merit although his works are spread across 19 galleries from Canada to Australia. Philip Wilson Steer, a Birkenhead lad, painted *The Beach at Walberswick* and *Girls Running: Walberswick Pier*, both of which are in the Tate. Don't bother looking for Walberswick Pier, will you?

George Orwell of *Nineteen Eighty-Four* fame lived here for a while but never did like the town. Then there was Derek Scott who worked on animating the Muppets, Val Parnell, and the actress Ann Todd who died at Walberswick.

✿ **Southwold Pier.** But there is a pier at Southwold. It was built to offer docking facilities to the paddle steamers which came up from London carrying holidaymakers to the piers at Southend, Clacton, Walton, Felixstowe, Southwold and Great Yarmouth. In 2000 the pier had a makeover and a small extension, ready for a more active life in the 21st century.

Southwold Fair. The combined attractions of a pier and a fair make this town unique among coastal resorts in East Anglia. Trinity Fair, held around three days at Whitsun, six Sundays after Easter, was traditionally opened by the Mayor from one of the carousels.

Henry IV gave the town its charter for a fair, so it is one of the longest-surviving in England. It has, of course, come a long way from its original use as a labour-exchange and market, and has been devoted to entertainment as long as anyone can remember.

THE SOUTHWOLD RAILWAY

The East Suffolk Railway carried the age of steam into coastal Suffolk, but had no intention of going close to the sea. It linked Woodbridge, and South Town Great Yarmouth via Saxmundham, Halesworth and Beccles. Branch lines were exploited by other companies and took track to Felixstowe, to Framlingham, to Snape Maltings, to Aldeburgh, and to Lowestoft. The Snape line was 1.4 miles long, carried barley in and malt out, 200 tons a year of the latter, was powered by horses and steam, and when it closed in 1960 it was still using track laid in 1859.

But what about the line to Southwold? When a local consortium raised the money, the decision was that the 8.75 miles of track would be on a three-foot gauge, narrower than the main line. There was an initial cost saving but there would always be the problem of transhipment at Halesworth, where the Southwold Railway was to meet the ESR, by then the Great Eastern.

Yet the building costs were £8,504 per mile, ridiculously expensive when one considers that there was only a moderate cutting on Southwold Common, no great embankments, and the only engineering was the single-track swing bridge over the Blyth near Southwold, a bridge which survives for walkers.

The SR was incorporated in 1876 and the line opened on 24 September 1879, roughly following the course of the Blyth River by Wenhaston, then making a tight loop around Blythburgh and heading towards Walberswick where it turned north-east. It crossed the river again near the confluence with Buss Creek, and ended by the main road; you can still see Railway Road in town.

There were three intermediate stations, and a later branch line from Southwold main station to the concrete quay. And there was a legend linking the town with the Woosung Railway in China, but the only connection was a Mr Jackson who brought some rails back from China; after all, Britain at that time was exporting railways worldwide.

The town museum has a model of a typical SR train, drawn by the 0-6-0 Wenhaston built in 1914 for the harbour line. Among the rolling stock were several six-wheel open goods wagons, two 4-wheel covered wagons and six 6-wheel carriages each 35ft long.

Despite its short line, the SR prospered, but sought a buy-out by the Great Eastern in 1894 but didn't like the offer.

The Blyth swing bridge was rebuilt in 1907, and records show that in 1908 there were more than 300 herring drifters based in town and mooring in Buss Creek; they used the railway to move their catch to Billingsgate. In 1910 the SR carried 12,824 tons of freight, mostly fish out, coal in, as well as 104,197 passengers, but now the GER declined to make an offer; it declined again in 1910.

After WW1, motor traffic began to encroach, and the fish catches were down. In 1928 Southwold Corporation allowed motor omnibuses to enter town and pick up passengers; that was the year when buses were allowed to go at 20mph, while the railway was permanently tied to 16mph.

The LNER, successor to the GER, offered to buy the SR in 1923 but once again the directors refused, although traffic was now on a steadily increasing decline , and when they begged the LNER to buy in 1929, they were turned down.

The Southwold Railway closed on 12 April 1929, its entire assets abandoned to the weather until 1941 when they were sold for scrap to help fight the Germans. The company was a financial mess and was liquidated on 19 April 1995.

OTHER VILLAGES:
WANGFORD. Wangford marks the site of a ford on the River Wang, unsurprisingly. In the mid-20th Century there were a dozen shops and several pubs, but the village is paying the same price that others are paying: isolation and commercial decline. The parish is home to members of the Ranulf-Fiennes,

Blythburgh Church

the Gilbey and the Eden families, with connections in exploration, gin and politics, but the famous ones do not live here. The church was part of the Cluniac Monastery, founded in 1160, the builders of the churches in Reydon and Southwold. Cluniacs? They were established in Cluny, Saône-et-Loire, in 910 and built their first English priory at Lewes in 1077. This priory was a satellite of the main one at Thetford.

BLYTHBURGH. Blythburgh has an *enormous*  church; you could probably squeeze half the village's houses into it; you could certainly pack the parishioners into a tiny corner. The nave is 127ft (38.6m) long so no wonder the place is called the Cathedral of the Marshes - the flood plain of the River Blyth which grows reeds a-plenty.

A church stood here from around 620, and we know it was in use soon after Alfred defeated Guthrum in 878. The present tower was built around 1330 - how?, one asks oneself. It lost its even more impressive steeple in 1577 when the Devil paid a call, and the 15th-cent nave took 80 years to complete.

William Dowsing - Cromwell's minion, you may recall - visited in April 1644 to order the churchwardens to strip out all the brasses and pay him for their labour: oh, yes, there were even more injustices then than there are today. He then fired lead shot into all the timberwork and when an angel's wing fell from the roof of the then-derelict building 200 years later, lead shot was picked out of it. Dowsing desecrated the place by stabling his horses in the church and by 1810 the large windows were bricked up, the carvings daubed with whitewash, and a brick column holding up part of the roof used a tomb as foundation.

By the 1870s the church was reopened for services, but the first congregations sat in the gloom under umbrellas. In 1881 a restoration fund was started and the place was fully open in 1884. Restoration work has continued almost unchecked ever since, with a major appeal in recent years to remove the ravages of the death-watch beetle.

❀ Jack-o'-the-Clock survived Dowsing, as did an alms-collecting box bearing the date 1473, originally called a Peter's Pence box. After the Reformation the farthings and pennies went to the local destitute instead of to Rome, but the European Union seems to have reversed the trend.

Devil. So why did the Devil pay that visit? In the guise of Black Shuck, the weird dog seen o'nights in the Eastern Counties (he who sees him dies, so beware), the Devil called on a Sunday in August 1577 during the reading of the second lesson. He struck the steeple and so felled it, then he sodainly gave a swing downe through ye church and there...slew two men and a lad...then he flew with wonderful force ...out of the church and on to Bungay where he killed two of that church's congregation.

Shuck takes his name from the Anglo-Saxon scucca, 'demon', and he had time to scratch his name on Blythburgh church door. You can easily mistake it for a lightning strike.Henry I gave the income from the original church to the

Fishing boats on Dunwich beach

abbot of St Osyth, near Clacton, but a later abbot used the local funds to establish an outpost back in Blythburgh; today it's called a priory but only a few fragments remain, on private land 200 yards north-east of the church, visible from the rear of the WI Hall.

And in 1412 Henry IV granted the abbot a licence to rebuild the church, a splendid return of favours.

At this time, Blythburgh was bustling. It had two charter fairs each year, a Mint, and a jail. It was at the lowest crossing point of the Blyth so mixed road traffic with river trade; today's mudflats all but fill the downstream lagoon but in the 12th Century there was adequate anchorage for the small vessels.

The river didn't enter the sea at its present mouth. It ran parallel but to the south, went south of Walberswick, then swung and headed south with a bit of west, across the Dingle Marshes, and joined the Dunwich River to reach the sea in that village, which had a good harbour. But the storm of 1328 blocked the Dunwich River mouth, spelling the beginning of the end for both communities. As Dunwich cliffs were eroded, the River Blyth became silted, and Blythburgh town's records note the receipt in 1478 "of 16d and no more" because the Bretons did not come that year with salt.

In 1590 the men of Southwold and Walberswick cut through the shingle bar and allowed the Blyth to enter the sea along its present course, but it was too late to save Blythburgh.

Toby's Walks. Tobias Gill, 'Black Toby', was a negro drummer in the Dragoons, stationed at Blythburgh in 1750. After an evening's booze he went for a walk and met Anne Blakemore (Blackmore) several miles from her Walberswick home. He is said to have raped and murdered her and he was convicted at Ipswich assizes, bound in chains and hanged at what is today's junction of the B1387 and A12, a mile south of Bly'burg on unconsecrated ground. And so his ghost haunts the spot, now a picnic site known as Toby's Walks.

Henham. The village of Henham is like Black Toby: it doesn't exist any more. But look in Wangford Church for a plaque which reads *John, first Earl of Stradbroke, Viscount Dunwich, Baron Rous and 6th Baronet.* The baronetcy was

Walberswick Green

created in 1660, the earldom in 1821, the First Earl being Viscount Dunwich.

The title lapsed, but a descendant was found running a sheep station in Australia - the present pseudo-earl. He came to Henham Hall and wanted to establish a nudist colony; he was filmed for television taking a bath in the grounds. When the locals protested, he settled for a traction engine rally for some years.

WALBERSWICK BEGAN LIFE as Wahlbertsvik or Waldbertsvik, the vik meaning either of two things: the Saxon word for a settlement, wìc, or the Viking word for an estuary, vik, from which the word Viking derives. You'll find Viken in Sweden, north of the Gulf of Bothnia. Wahlbert was the Saxon who founded the settlement yet the Vikings certainly sailed up the estuary, which in those days - you recall? - entered the sea at Dunwich. Presumably Walberswick was on a bend in the Blyth River, for if the known erosion at Dunwich is anything to go by, the North Sea was a couple of miles further east. You could walk from Walberswick to the fishing sheds which, centuries later, were to be the first buildings of Southwold.

Fishing? There's now a crab-catching contest held every summer. The crabs are returned to the water alive.

Charters. Whatever its name, the town received its first charter in 1262 from Henry III, with later charters in 1483 from Richard III, in 1485 from the new Henry VII, in 1553 from Edward VI, in 1558 from Mary, and finally in 1625 from the new Charles I; six charters, for a town with around a thousand people today. Most of the charters were to grant exemption from tolls and taxes to the town's tradesmen and merchants - a little tax haven on the Suffolk coast!

This favourable if unfair treatment helped the town to prosper in importing timber, salt and coal, and exporting fish, cereals and wool. In return, the Crown received an annual gift of fish, a practice common on the east coast.

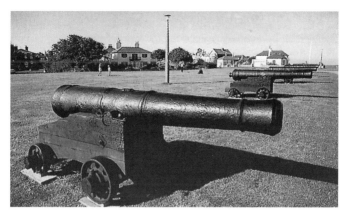

Gun Cliff, Southwold

The Walberswick charters were in effect countering the power of Dunwich which, before erosion attacked it, controlled all trade on the river; a charter of 1230 had granted the Dunwich burghers the right to charge tolls on cargos for Walberswick and Blythburgh, which frequently resulted in the towns going to battle with each other.

Tolls. Eventually Sir Robert Swillington, the Lord of Blythburgh, which then included Walberswick, held a fair on the marshes between Walberswick and Dunwich. This action, combined with the refusal to pay Dunwich's demanded tolls, brought the matter to the notice of Richard II. In 1400 Richard's successor, Henry IV, ordered an inquiry which laboured for eight years before allowing Sir Richard's lawyers to prove that Dunwich's claim to the tolls was false. Taken with the great storm, it was the beginning of the end of Dunwich's glory.

But the town didn't give in easily. Four years later the arguments had resorted to violence once more when one Thomas Clerk, leading a group of armed men, prevented a Dutch ship from docking at Blythburgh.

Iceland. Records show that in 1451 Wahlbert's former town had 13 ships trading with the Faeroes, with Iceland, and across the North Sea with Scandinavia and the Low Countries. In 1597 the duty was 3/4d - three-and-fourpence or 16.7p - on every voyage to Iceland, and 2d (1p) on every cargo of cheese. These duties were paid to the churchwardens and stayed in the town, while most taxes at that time went to the local nobility and so to the Crown. The Church raised its income directly from the parishioners as a tithe, or a tenth of everything they produced; every tenth sheaf of corn, every tenth pig, every tenth herring. Gradually this tithe was converted to a cash payment and eventually it became a property tax additional to the rates, but at far less than 10%.

St Andrew. Walberswick town must have been first rate as it had two churches concurrently since Saxon times...so what, you may say: Dunwich started with nine! Worbelswick's first church, on the shore, was demolished in 1473 (but Dunwich lost its first in 1320), leaving the second, ❂ St Andrew's, in the process of being rebuilt. The tower was planned in 1426 with its builders, working in summer only - some were fishermen in winter - receiving each year 𝔴𝔬 𝔰𝔥𝔢𝔢𝔩𝔶𝔫𝔤𝔰 𝔬𝔣 𝔩𝔞𝔲𝔤𝔥𝔣𝔲𝔩 𝔪𝔬𝔫𝔢𝔶 𝔬𝔣 𝔍𝔫𝔤𝔩𝔬𝔫𝔡; 𝔞𝔫𝔡 𝔞 𝔠𝔞𝔡𝔢 𝔣𝔲𝔩𝔩 𝔬𝔣 𝔥𝔢𝔯𝔯𝔶𝔫𝔤𝔢, or 40/- (£2) of lawful money of England and 100 herring.

By 1493 the ❂ tower was complete, reaching 90ft (27m) and forming a suitable landmark for sailors, as well as a lookout for possible invaders. The original small nave had been destroyed around 1480, leaving the town without adequate provision for prayer, but the new nave, whose shell is seen today, was far larger and in keeping with a community as wealthy as Walberswick then was.

Silt. But the town's prosperity was already coming under threat; this was the time when Blythburgh was struggling for survival as its river was silting; the original mouth had been blocked by that great storm in 1328 and the river had carved itself a new exit to the sea into Dunwich harbour. Dunwich, having lost four of its nine churches to erosion, was suffering from the silting of its own harbour as its coast eroded. In truth, the fate of all three towns rested on the ability of the little river to carry ships, and the Blyth was losing that battle. It didn't help that ships were getting bigger.

Black Death. Bubonic plague struck the east coast early in 1349, killing almost half the population, devastating the economy and weakening the social structure of the nation. Within half a century bondsmen could buy their freedom from servitude for 6/8d - 33p or half a mark - plus a favour to the town; this is the origin of granting someone the freedom of the borough.

Henry VIII. In London, Henry VIII grew tired of his wife Catherine of Aragon and sought a divorce. Cardinal Wolsey engineered the split with Rome with just a few personal problems such as a spell in prison. Henry denounced the Roman church because of its stand against divorce, protested so vehemently that he became the original Protestant, an act which gave rise to the Church of England, then he took as his second wife the Norfolk-born Anne Boleyn. In 1534 he had himself appointed head of the new Anglican Church, a position the Monarch has held ever since.

In his fury, he began the mass destruction of almost all Catholic institutions, notably the abbeys, priories, convents and nunneries, and so changed the face of England. **Blythburgh Abbey** was among the victims, and in Walberswick the church lost its income, a violation master-minded by Sir Arthur Hopton of Westwood Lodge. This loss gave another stimulus to the economic decline as most of the church's income had been spent in Walberswick - although, as we have seen, Blythburgh (and other places) gave alms income to Rome. That, of course, would have to stop - quite rightly.

The churchwardens sold the great bell in 1585, its 1,707lb (774kg) of metal raising £26.8.9d. The next year fire destroyed part of the town, reducing it to 54 families, and after more fires in 1633, 1683 and 1749, Walberswick was down to 20 houses and 100 people. Part of the trouble was that thatch was so relatively cheap, and tiles so expensive. Cutting the new mouth for the river in 1590 had merely slowed the collapse of the economy, and had been more beneficial to the people of Southwold.

Vanishing church. Shrinking Walberswick could no longer afford its massive church. After more than a century without repairs, the townspeople began to dismantle the nave in June 1695, using the rubble to build a much smaller nave, just 64ft long, inside the original. The churchwardens sold the remaining three bells, the roof lead and the timber for £303.1.11d, offsetting the cost of the new nave at £291.8.9d.

Westwood Lodge. Midway between Blythburgh and Walberswick stands Sir Arthur Hopton's former home, empty for years after the death of its modern-times owner, but occupied again in the 1990s. Empty, that is, except for the ghost of a woman in a long white dress. A few days after a gamekeeper claimed to have seen her, three policemen kept vigil in the house one night in October 1972 and experienced a sudden chilling of the air. They recorded noises which they couldn't explain, and their ghost traps were disturbed, but they never saw anything.

In other times Westwood Lodge was the family seat of the Blois family (pronounced *bloyz*); they were neighbours of the Barn family whom we will meet at Dunwich. The lodge has an unusual feature in its design as the outer wall is doubled, leaving a narrow passage inside through which the servants were expected to walk, so that they were not seen by the gentry. As I've not been inside I don't know what happens with the windows.

Mackintosh. Charles Rennie Mackintosh was Walberswick's best-known artist, but his stay in the village was controversial. He was born in Glasgow in 1868 and studied at

St. Jame's Church, Dunwich

the Glasgow School of Art to become a decorator and architect. His ideas were controversial even then; he claimed that furniture should be designed in straight lines and right-angles, and he developed this idea to the point of being the first exponent in Britain of Art Nouveau.

He quit Glasgow for good in 1914 and moved to Walberswick where his career finally moved from architecture to art and literature. He was planning to write another book in German, not a wise thing to do with the Great War about to begin.

Some time later he was walking along the dunes by Walberswick with German and Austrian friends, studying and painting the wild flowers, when the police arrested him on a charge of spying. After he talked his way out of the cells he left the village, never to return. In 1920 he retired to Port-Vendres by the French Pyrenees where he eventually concentrated on water colours, but he came back to London where he died on 10 December 1928.

DUNWICH

WHAT A TINY place Dunwich is! There's a gently-

National Trust Cottages, Dunwich Heath

sloping hill from the crossroads, where there's the church, the rebuilt ruins of an earlier church, and a leper colony. Then come the few houses on the south side of the street, mixed with the museum and a pub. At the bottom the road turns right and there are a few further houses. There's a short track to some fishing huts, to a car park big enough to hold the entire population several hundred times, and a fish-and-chip shop with a big reputation.

Could this once have been a Roman port with a large sheltered harbour? Could it have had nine churches? Could it have been the seat of a bishopric that took in all of East Anglia? Could it have been an important shipbuilding city? Could it have been the capital city of the Danelaw, stretching west to Northampton? Could it have been a major fishing port? Could it have in more recent times sent two Members to Parliament? Could it have played a part in the creation of Downing College in Cambridge?

The answer to these eight questions is: yes. And the reason why Dunwich fell from importance is simple: erosion.

The Danish king Guthrum or Goturm has a place in history: there's a cave in Shetland called Goturm's Hole, where the king hid on his way to England, and his reign ended when Alfred the Great defeated him in England's first recorded naval battle - off Shotley in Harwich Harbour; the place is known as Bloody Point. But it was he who created Dunwich as his capital city.

Norman Conquest. After 1066 the city prospered further and by the 12th century it was one of England's main ports, not far behind London and Bristol. Domesday records 500 tenants and 80 burgesses, giving an estimated population, with descendants, of 3,000.

King John (1199-1216) gave it its first charter, with rights over all east coast wrecks, in return for an annual fee of 5,000 eels. The thriving shipbuilding industry came in the 13th century, by which time the city's nine parishes were well established each with its church. Around now the population may have reached its peak at some 6,000.

The cruel sea. The sea had always been a threat, continually eroding the shoreline as it has done since the retreat of the Ice Age but don't forget that the east coast has always been sinking.

It eroded westward, and didn't stop because Dunwich was

Minsmere "scrape" is home to avocets

29

in its way. In 1328 there came that storm which blocked the mouth of the Blyth and the Dunwich River. Yet St Leonard's Church had vanished into the sea in 1320, St Martin's in 1340 and St Katherine's around 1350. It is recorded that in 1408 six men were hired to watch the harbour defences at dangerous high tides, especially at night, but by now most of the depleted population was living in the central parishes of St John, St Peter and All Saints. The town's ❀ **museum** records all this in splendid detail; look for the anchor standing outside.

Despite erosion, the fishing fleet continued to prosper, paying more than £18 in taxes in 1407 for its catch of sprat, herring and mackerel. Cod fishing in Icelandic waters was soon to begin as the herring shoals started to decline.

Erosion elsewhere. Erosion redraws the coastline of East Anglia on an almost annual basis. The current comes down the east coast and on its way has created the Yorkshire peninsula of Holderness. It hits the Norfolk coast, forming a lesser current which flows west, creating the sandbars of Blakeney Point and Scolt Head and gradually filling in The Wash. But the main current flows east and scours away the coast, making Cromer to Gt. Yarmouth the easiest part of the map of England to draw freehand.

Lost bells. Beyond Yarmouth, you can see the peninsula opposite Gorleston and the vast shingle bank of Orford Ness, both pointing southward. Then there's Landguard Point off Felixstowe, and the erosion at Walton-on-the-Naze. You'll have heard the legend which says that on stormy nights you can hear the lost church bells of Dunwich ringing under water. A nice saying but, if those bells still have clappers, they'll be tolling from Orford Ness.

Rotten Borough. Lawyers and politicians had also prospered in Dunwich's glory days; there was even less to choose between the two professions than there is today. Dunwich had been a parliamentary borough for some generations, returning *two* members to Parliament; for example, in the fifty-day session of 1410, Peter Codon and William Barbour were the MPs, each receiving £9.0.6d Late in the century the MPs had to take their pay in herring as the town was so poor.

St John's Church vanished around 1540, but the next victim hung on until 1712-1725. Blackfriars Monastery, the Templars' Church of St Margaret & John the Baptist, and the Chapel of St Francis, went in the 19th century, and All Saints, abandoned in the 1750s, slipped over the cliff edge between 1903 and 1919. Its last ❀ buttress was saved and has been rebuilt near the new ❀ Church of St James, by the remains of the ❀ leper colony.

Downing Street. George Downing wanted to be an MP. The Cambridge voters spurned him so he bought property in Dunwich in 1708 and stood for election in 1710. He brought in 81 traders from outside the borough and made them Freemen of Dunwich; naturally they voted him into office. Queen Anne's death in 1712 prompted another election - there was always a new government with a new monarch - and the freemen arranged there would be no opposition to Downing and his fellow, Sir Kenneth Kemp - so they were re-elected.

In the 1715 poll Field Marshal Sir Robert Rich and Colonel Long of Saxmundham were nominated as the polls opened , according to custom, and Downing and Kemp were defeated. In 1720, Downing gave his tenant freemen notice to quit, so Long built them cottages: Long Row is still in the village. Kemp sold out to Downing, who now owned two thirds of Dunwich and so controlled the votes. The army officers were defeated and Downing sold the second seat to Miles Barn for £1,200, for one Parliament only. So Dunwich was now a pocket borough - in Downing's pocket. Intrigue continued past Downing's death and Barn and partner held their seats until the Reform Act of 1832. Some of the Barn family still come back to Dunwich for a sentimental visit.

College and street. The Attorney General was a trustee of Sir George Downing's will and used his authority to settle some money on the founding of a college at Cambridge University - Downing College. Another member of the family gave some London property to the Prime Minister of the day. The grand house was number ten in the street, which was renamed in Sir George's honour - Downing Street.

❀ **Dunwich Heath.** South of the village is the 213-acre heath, the last bit of what may have been farmland created in Neolithic times; it was given to the National Trust in 1968. On the skyline are the ❀ Coastguard Cottages, built in 1827 for watching smugglers. They now house tearooms, a gift shop and three holiday cottages, while the Heath Barn is where students of all ages learn about wildlife and conservation.

❀ **Minsmere.** When the Germans were threatening invasion the Government arranged for the Minsmere saltings to be flooded. By the end of the war, nature had taken over and the Minsmere reserve had virtually formed itself. In 1947 the RSPB took it over and has made many improvements, adding hides, trails and an information centre, so that now the heath, an Area of Outstanding Natural Beauty, is home to avocets, bitterns, marsh and hen harriers, barn owls, dartford warblers and nightjars, among other birds, as well as to muntjac. This second-largest of England's reedbeds - Walberswick has the largest - is now one of the major reserves in the country, a home for creatures that have changed little in a thousand years, breeding within sight of one of mankind's latest marvels: the ❀ Sizewell Nuclear Reactors.